BATTLE SCARS

SHRIYA PHADKE

Battle Scars
Copyright © 2023, Shriya Phadke

Published by Books That Matter
New York / Oklahoma
All rights reserved.

No part of this publication may be reproduced, stored in a retrieval system, stored in a database and/or published in any form or by any means, electronic, mechanical, photocopying, recording or otherwise, without the prior written permission of the publisher.

Paperback ISBN 978-1-61343-138-2

*This one's for you. Yes, you.
You and all the different versions of you.
The one that loves, the one that protects,
the one that hurts and even the one that hates.
Every single part of your being, will find itself
concealed between these pages, and I hope,
once you find yourself, you'll help others
find themselves too.*

In other people's words, you'll find yourself again, and again.

- **Soman Chainani**

Contents

Preface   3

Paper cut   4

2.1 Lo(ve)ss   22

2.2 Senses   44

Itisnevertheend   52

About the Author   58

Preface

To those who broke me, played me, stabbed me and
betrayed me, you simply succeeded in trying.
For I licked my wounds, and stood my ground and all I
have to say is
look at me now.
However,
I forgive you.
I hope you learn to do the same.

I
Paper cut

Delicate, but once it cuts you, the pain overpowers.

Sometimes I ask myself, would my younger self be proud of me?
Then I realize,
I am more proud
of my younger self than she would ever be of me now.

- *Nostalgia*

I wish I could cry so loud
that the whole world would shake
 but not a single soul
would hear a single sound

- Sound of Silence

You say you hurt them
because you love them,
but I don't believe you.
I think you hurt them
because you need them to feel
the hurting that's happening inside of you,
The twinge of the blade slicing into your soul,
lacerating your bruised heart
Into two,
because you believe
that this infliction of pain upon your beloved
will cure your own.

- The thin line between love and hurt

He didn't call me for dinner that day.
He never calls me for dinner
On the days when he feels,
I am in the wrong.
In sooth,
He doesn't call me for dinner,
Because he doesn't want to see the face,
Of the person he himself wronged,
And feel that twisting guilt,
Tugging at his heart.

Father bought son a skateboard
So son could feel the wind in his hair
And ride through the joys of life,
like in the happy endings
of children's cartoons.
Father rode on daughter's back like a skateboard
and pushed her so fast.
They both crashed
Except,
He got back up again,
While daughter was left
Broken in two
Forever irreparable.
His daughter no longer
His broken skateboard
Forevermore.

- *Skateboard*

I tried to weep,
but there were no tears left to cry.
So I moved on.
And when the tears filled back up,
I didn't shed a single one.

I don't belong to you.
I am not the chair you crashed onto
That day,
Or the door you broke.
I am not a doll
Who'll go unscathed
From the bloody whips
Of your words.
I am a creature who feels.
I will feel
The dissipating love
Taste
The unintentional,
sour words
Leave my mouth.
Smell
The rusting metallic red
From the barcodes on my arms.
I will feel it all.
Just as you felt
When you broke that door.

I wish I could cry so loud
That the whole world would thunder,
Yet no one would hear a sound.

You drank up
another's' love
but you never filled it back up.
Now left,
empty and barren,
The sun dried her up.
-*What is a heart
without something there to break it?*

When I tried to cry you back,
The tears simply created
Pools of my own reflection.
Dotted with red,
I knew.
The fault was mine.

I am angry,
All of the time.
It is easier to be angry,
than anything else,
because it hurts the least.
You have power;
Adrenaline coursing through your veins,
The sound of its speed
Beating in your ears,
Deafening you.
So, you say the wrong things,
but at the right time.
But the Achilles heel,
is that you have no control.
And every time I get angry,
I lose control.

They say we hurt to love
When in reality,
We love to hurt.

Loneliness
is like sleeping in pitch darkness
with the sound of silence.
Every muscle in your body
aches for the gentle graze
And comforting embrace
Of human contact.
Yet even if they're there
you are invisible
because they choose not to see you.

Atlas

You put all this weight on my shoulders
Forgetting that I am not Atlas.
I am simply a speck of dust
Trying to navigate my way
Through this sandstorm
We call life.
Yet still,
You hurl your pains,
Your ailments and your ugliest desires
And expect me
To carry your bruised world,
The way Atlas carries ours.
But instead, I shudder.
Shoulders breaking, I submerge
Into your rubble,
Succumbing
To the gravity
Of my mind.

Barcodes

When my arm begins to bleed I get lost inside the cuts.
I find myself in a new world,
distanced from their agony inflicted upon me.
I should be lost within the vein
and the muscle and the plasma
And the red
when in actuality,
I am found.
I peer into the depths
of the gashes on my wrist
and find the glowing part of me
that I always seem to lose.
Which is why
when suffering
I go on a journey.
Blade to skin;
The perpetrator penetrating
Impaling the vein,
Bleeding the pain away.
This journey
Is in search of that part of me
that makes me whole
once more.

She will only listen to the silence in your screams
and the silence
in your silence,
but she will never listen to the sound
of your own voice
Echoing in between.
A void she chooses
To deafen herself too.

I've searched the whole world
I've looked above and beyond
Yet in a sea full of oysters
There's not a single pearl to be found.
My heart beats for two,
No consent, 6 feet down.
You broke my door and waited
Till it was beyond repair
To buy new screws.
Hope is another sugar coat.
I know you meant well
But if hiding did me better
Why would I give in to your concerns
to fix my house

II

Lo(ve)ss

What is a heart without something there to break it?

What am I to you? I ask.
You are the rush of blood
filling every crevice,
every nook and cranny of my heart,
beating it back to life.
He says

The sun cannot set,
without a moon ready to rise.
Just as I will fight sleep,
till you shine like a star.

My heart dwells on the past, the present,
people it shouldn't,
things it shouldn't,
But at the end of the day,
It'll always choose yours.

Tears, bold and bright streamed down my face
The darkness enveloped me,
I felt so out of place.
My feet were on the edge, quivering with fear
With a sigh I asked myself,
"what am I even doing here."
The world was spinning, I jolted, stepping back
Maybe I should stand up and
fix the crack
My heart's too weak,
I can't fathom any other reality
It's time for me to say goodbye
to my dejected mentality.
I prepare myself,
wind ricocheting off of my face
The tears have fallen,
it's time to close the case.
One foot off, I feel the weight
cascading down,
The other one follows,
leaving without a frown.
I'm soaring downward,
my hair in a vertical mess
I can't think straight,
it's too late to second guess.

Numbness re-fills me,
tickling my chest,
The voices begin to silence,
signaling the end of my quest.
Finally prepared, I begin to let myself fly,
Unable to realize
how I could have ever said goodbye.
Still falling, I feel my eyes begin to close,
Until suddenly,
an angel appears, superimposed.
A parachute, bright and strong,
Lifts me up,
as if there was nothing wrong.
I feel the weight on my shoulders
re appear,
But this time it's painless
and a little more clear.
My eyes flutter open,
awaken from their slumber
The pain and guilt arise,
beginning to encumber.
The parachute lifts me higher,
through the bright blue sky
I no longer feel the pit in my stomach,
feeling so much more
alive.

As I reach the platform,
my eyes become misty
Overwhelmed with emotion,
my heart was a little twisty.
The angel dropped me off,
a smile appearing on my face,
It was a special moment,
as the smile felt out of place.
The guilt was gone,
and so was the pain
I was finding myself,
all over again.
The parachute stayed with me,
to help when I tried to fall
But after the first time, it stood stationary,
doing nothing at all.
Its presence made me feel alive,
bringing back the light
to my soul
Together as one,
I knew we would get
through it after all.

For years ahead,
we stood tall together,
Through the ups and downs,
and even through bad weather.
But the one thing I will remember,
even after it all,
It was there, the first time I tried to fall.

He smells like sweet earth,
Like a garden on a rainy day
Like flowers on a moonlit night,
When the sun would be far away.
His skin glows in the darkness,
Radiating in the twilight,
His eyes are just as beautiful,
Calloused yet ever so bright.
His tan skin like desert sand,
Bears the inconspicuous scars
Blind to sight, but visible to touch.
You would find him wandering the meadows
On a sunny afternoon,
When nobody is around
And the clouds cast down their shadows.
He's a sight for sore eyes
You would find him in a polaroid picture
But whenever he's not around
I feel as if I had to say goodbye.
He smells like rainy days and strawberry pie
You would find him in a sunlit room
But what you might not know is that
He means everything to me.

When you look at me,
I feel transparent;
your eyes ablaze with passion.
When your hand brushes against mine,
electricity zaps through my body.
Break my heart.
Rip it to shreds
just to put it back together
and rip it again.
It will always belong to you.
every inch,
every crevice and every naked truth
belongs to you.

Autumn leaves fell as the winter snow stood idle.
I noticed as I fell,
the note in my back pocket
My withered dreams were mending
My beaten hope was waiting
For a message or a sign from you.
The solitude I loathed, I was longing for once more.
I was told to be happy, but I was hungry for more
So I took what wasn't meant for me
with so much greed and
Selfishly
I lost all the respect I'd earned
faster than I'd gained.
It is what they think of me, what they say,
when my back is turned.
It's those assumptions that hurt most
when your friends are the ones behind the phone.
So please, if you see me soon,
Be careful of breaking my unfixed heart
Because far too many times
I've had it broken like a fool.

Our twisted fate
can only be unwound
by the release
of your strangling hands
from my pulsating heart.
But what if
I do not want to unwind it?

It is difficult to tell you how much I love you,
So I will say this:
My love for you
is like a blanket.
I will keep you warm
When the air gets cold.
My cool spring perfume
Filling your nostrils,
giving you comfort.
I will be there for you
when you reach your bed
alone and afraid,
to embrace you.
I will protect you from the voices
outside your bedroom door.
I will love you
till my fabric tears and wears.
I am not just a blanket,
I am your blanket,
and will forever be
your blanket.

I saw you in a picture frame
gleaming under the warm undertones
of the lamp we bought
when we were 16.
I saw you in a picture frame,
your hair tinted brown like autumn;
your smile sweet and kind.
I saw you in a picture frame.
Your hand wrapped around my shoulder,
as you looked into my eyes,
staring into my soul,
touching my heart.
I saw you in a picture frame,
the moment before our last.

You are my drug;
I will love you till it kills me.

She was love, he was fate.
They met each other at the gate.
Every night she would come and go
And find him standing all alone
At the gate.
One day she came,
And found herself all alone
For she was love and he was fate,
And fate isn't always kind,
As he stood on the other side
Of the gate.

I wish I didn't take it that far.
I wish I was still sitting in the backseat of your car
Tell me a lie
Because the truth is I could never
say you were mine
I miss you
Everyday of my life.
I miss your eyes and even the way we fight
So don't tell me
you'll always choose her
Because I'd choose you every single time.
We'd light up the sky
You'd say you'd be mine forever
You told me
We would be fine
My mistake was believing
You were right
I even wrote you a love song
But I know you'd never do the same for me
And I turned out to be right.
We danced and you put my hands in yours and you said
We would be alright.
But we were never alright.

To push them away
Is to forget, but not to forgive
And to let them go
Is to forgive, but be forced to forget
The joys and the smiles
The look in their eyes
The memories.
The bittersweet, beautiful memories.
So one day,
Even if you push me away
Even if you cannot forgive me just yet,
Never let me go.

Maybe if I was beautiful,
He would love me back.
Maybe if I was wiser,
They wouldn't be saying that.
If only the world,
Was my oyster,
Maybe then they would finally love me for who I am.
Maybe I'm too honest,
They always sell me short.
Maybe I'm overzealous,
Or an excuse of a last resort.
They can't seem to see I'm delicate,
I'm struggling to find myself.
"Maybe if I was beautiful…"
Or maybe I'm just inadequate.

I don't usually believe in "ever afters,"
But ours will be
the greatest love story ever told.
For it wasn't I
who walked into your tale,
Or you into mine.
We
Walked into ours'

Inspired by Soman Chainani's "The school for Good and Evil" series

One day,
you'll spread your wings
and fly out of the nest.
But when you fall
and crash onto
 the hard earth below,
You will find me ready
 to catch you
and to bind your wounds
before I let you go once more
 to try again.

I WANT THE MOONLIGHT TO SHINE ON ME WRAPPED UP IN YOUR ARMS AS WE SLEEP UNDER THE STARS THROUGH THE CHILLY NIGHT. I WANT TO WAKE UP, TANGLED IN THE SHEETS, SEEING THE REFLECTION OF YOUR SMILE THROUGH THE MIRROR BEHIND MY DOOR, JUST TO DO IT ALL OVER AGAIN.

III

Senses

Seeing you is not enough, but this will be

Touch

Feel the palm of my hand
and trace it all the way to my heart
so you know
that every inch belongs to you.
Feel my lips on yours,
so you know
My kisses do too.
Feel my forehead
touching yours
as I look into your eyes
So you know
I love you.
Then, I'll feel your arms
wrapping around me
When I know
That you love me too

Human touch;
Benign yet detrimental.
But I couldn't care less. I'll risk it,
if it means it is his touch, I earn in return.

Smell

You
Smell like lavender in the rain
like midnight winters
and warm hands touching warm hearts
You smell like solar eclipses
and anti climactic romance movies.
But most of all,
you smell of love.
Soft, yearning love,
that belongs to me.

Taste

Your minty taste
Tickles and dances
on the tip of my tongue
long after your lips
have touched mine.

Sound

Your enigmatic laughter
Radiates life
Back into my desolation.
You have a voice like a hummingbird;
Delicate and sweet
That tickles the ear
And flutters the heart.
But my most favorite sound
Is your heartbeat
Echoing into mine,
Beating it back to life;
A symphony of enamor.

Sight

Arjuna's guru asked him
What do you see
upon that tree?
He replied,
I see the eye of the bird
and the eye only,
as he shot his arrow,
a perfect aim.
I am not a powerful warrior,
or a learned teacher.
I am simply a pair of eyes staring into another.
Ones that are blue like the ocean
and green like the forest,
And sensitive like sparrows,
Yet strong like Arjuna's arrow,
hoping they will light up for me
the way I light up
for them.

IV

Itisneverthend

Snowflakes dance down,
The air, crisp as paper.
The smell of fresh earth fills my nostrils as I inhale.
The tops of trees blanketed with white
The wind blows through me, sending chills down my spine.
The meadow is empty, feeling vast and wide,
I stand in the center of it all, the world passing me by.
Rabbits gallop past, inconspicuous in the foot deep snow,
As the echoes of birds chirping fills the surrounding silence.
I stand with my eyes closed, at peace with the world around me,
With everything in balance, dancing in harmony.
I never want to leave
This heaven on earth,
But as all things do, this too will come to an end.
Careful not to trip, I gently walk back home,
one foot, In front of the other,
My heart, warm and fluttery like the birds.
Winter has come,
Just as quick, it will go
But in my heart it will stay forever
Keeping me cozy when dark times unfurl.

If you fear something, don't cower from it.
Instead,
make friends with it.

The room feels empty
Walls so bleak
I can't unsee it
Can't even speak
But I'm not afraid anymore
Although I do seem unsure.
The papers rotting
Posters down
I can't pinpoint it
Can't erase the frown
But I'm not afraid anymore
Although I do seem unsure.
Packed your baggage
Burned it down
Can't escape it
Can't let it out
But I'm not afraid anymore
Although I do seem unsure.
Bloody paper
On the floor
Holds my pain from
When you walked out the door
But I'm not afraid anymore
Although I do seem unsure.

Time
What a fickle thing.
Invisible to sight,
Invincible against turning back,
Though we yearn to do just that.
We foolishly waste,
The limited amount we have been anointed
And then ask for more,
Though we never get what we wish for.
Through this soliloquy I try to say,
Don't waste the 24 hours you have in your day.
Save some, spend some,
and share some with loved ones
For they too have fleeting lives.
As time is of the essence,
Get up and go do
what you've been procrastinating,
Because time waits for no one,
So don't be left behind.

end.

About the Author

To pay homage to *Battle Scars*, this is me in verse.

I am a Haagen Dazs ice cream
I am the smell of imminent snow at the first signs of December
I am 'stargazing' and then stealing the north star
To put upon a Christmas tree
I am Sunflower Vol.6 by Harry Styles
I am a C sharp; Dramatic yet gentle and soft
I am love, but I am also hurt, because I love just as strongly as I feel hurt.
I "break a leg",
Standing tall upon a stage.
I am music; my voice is the sound of music
I am theatre; Through fantastical worlds, I can truly be
I am literature; Life develops meaning with a sense of imagination

I am a daydreamer; Dreaming about dreams becoming my life

And sometimes falling in love.

I am an unfinished book
With so much already filling the pages,
This book is Shriya
And Shriya will write
till the cream color of the pages
are filled with flamboyant ink,
Because she still has
So much more to share.

www.ingramcontent.com/pod-product-compliance
Lightning Source LLC
Chambersburg PA
CBHW042340150426
43195CB00006B/117